THE COLLEGE GRADUATE'S SURVIVAL GUIDE

To our parents,
This is perhaps the most expensive
book you will ever hold.
Read it . . . slowly.
Enjoy it . . . immensely.
Thanks . . . a lot.

Illustrations by Rick Penn-Kraus

Copyright © 1987 by Larry Cohen,
Steve Zweig and Caren Rubin
Illustrations copyright © 1987 by Price Stern Sloan, Inc.
Published by PRICE STERN SLOAN, Inc.
360 North La Cienega Boulevard, Los Angeles, California 90048

ISBN: 0-8431-2207-2

THE COLLEGE GRADUATE'S $URVIVAL GUIDE

by Larry Cohen, Steve Zweig,
and Caren Rubin

PRICE STERN SLOAN, INC.
Los Angeles

TABLE OF CONTENTS

Foreword

1 A MINOR WORD ABOUT MAJORS

or "What kind of a job can you get
with *that*?"............................13

2 SO THIS IS REAL LIFE

or "I didn't spend $50,000 for you to be a..."...21

3 THE 20-MINUTE WELCOME HOME

or "We're doing this for your own good..."....31

4 HELP WANTED

or "I hear Aunt Sally's brother's cousin's
husband is looking for someone. Why don't
you call?"............................37

**5 GETTING IN THE DOOR, WINDOW OR
EXECUTIVE WASHROOM**

or "Mom, where did you put that
graduation outfit?"........................43

6 THE GIFT OF CABLE

or "I'll do it during the first commercial..."....49

7 ODD JOBS AND THE COLLEGE EGO

or "There's only one place you can
go...up!"................................. 57

8 FOOD FOR THOUGHT

or "If you think this is a restaurant...tip!"....65

9 HOME SWEET HOME

or "It's what they call a 'fixer upper' ".........75

**10 TIME, MONEY AND OTHER
THINGS YOU'RE SHORT OF**

or " 'Tis better to give than to receive,
but in your case..."........................83

**11 COLLEGE GRADUATES & OTHER
HAZARDS OF SEX**

or "Stop me if you've heard this...".......... 89

12 CH-CH-CH-CH-CHANGES

or "Can I quote you on that?".............. 93

Afterword

This book is more than funny—it's true. If it had been available when I graduated, it would have convinced me to do the only sane thing—go to graduate school.

–Bruce Feirstein

(Author of REAL MEN DON'T EAT QUICHE and NICE GUYS SLEEP ALONE)

FOREWORD

So, finding a job isn't going to be as easy as you thought, is it? Especially one you want. Sure you've got the degree, but now what? Let's face it, everyone has a degree these days. I mean you got one, so how tough could it have been? The only difference between a college degree today and a high school diploma twenty years ago is the $50,000 price tag. You're probably thinking to yourself at this point, "I should have taken the fifty grand and tried my chances with a McDonald's franchise." You're right! You should have, but you didn't. Now, the "help wanted" sign out front seems to mock you personally as you walk by. The "over 50 billion served" sign isn't helping either. What's past is past. At present you're broke, living in your old room, responding to remarks such as, "Get out of the house, and get a life, bum," and being introduced as "the help."

But . . . you're a college graduate. You know how to think on your feet. You've got your education, your degree, your school's reputation, your ambition and an ego so big it requires its own living space. You know you're different, a cut above. Somehow you know you've got that something special. Sure you do. WAKE UP! Special is a relative term, and unless your relatives are hiring, you're no more special than every other aging adolescent with a degree. The guy at the corner 7-11 probably has a Ph.D. in Linguistics. After all, it's not easy to find someone who can say cherry slurpee in thirteen languages. Thus we see that higher education does pay off. Currently it pays $3.35 an hour for part-time work.

Of course, upon leaving college many graduates are accompanied by what is known as the "college ego." (See chapter 7.) It is just this inflated sense of competence that has pushed many graduates to search for that one certain job. The one for which they've been specifically bred. Some of those oversized aspirations may be realized if you are able to secure any of the following:

>•**CEO of a multinational corporation**—Being a titular figurehead is great. Responsibilities are kept to a minimum and the hours are wonderful. Everyone knows the Chief Financial Officer is the guy who actually runs the company. Except when the company's so big, it runs itself. Just keep yourself looking busy and stay out of the way.

>•**Chief Justice of the Supreme Court**—The ideal position for the graduate with an acutely developed Messiah complex. Your two basic responsibilities include keeping your robe clean and pressed, and bringing doughnuts once every nine days.

•**College President**—Your principal duties are appeasing all major donors, slowly phasing out financial aid, and reassuring the student body that even with the thirteen percent tuition hike, the college will still be losing money. Previous experience as a T.V. evangelist is helpful.

Of course the aforementioned positions tend to be snapped up quickly. This means that for most of you this next year may prove a bit more difficult than you had anticipated. A year of trial and error, heavy on the error, is standard procedure. If you were smart you would have majored in persistence and minored in sucking up.

You really have your work cut out for you and you are going to need all the help you can get. That's where we come in. This book is designed to assist the recent college graduate through that first fun-filled year of real life:

> **Real life:** (*re* al leif), n. when bills come to you directly and not to your parents; when you can't schedule your job to begin after 11 a.m.; when social security checks are not mouthwash and deodorant in the morning; when homework takes on the startling definition of work to actually be done at home. Not on the way to class.

Yes. Real life. Remember that nebulous looming threat you always believed to be a figment of your parents' imaginations? You're finally there.

So between employers knocking your door down to offer you executive positions, flip through the pages of this guide and learn from the wisdom of three seasoned college graduates. Okay, two grads and a third who could operate the electric typewriter.

For those of you who are a bit apprehensive about diving into this book so shortly after graduation, have no fear. While reading about stress interviews and cooking for yourself may sound nightmarish, we promise to make it a learning experience similar to your favorite beer . . . lite, less filling and a third fewer pages than a regular book.

We assure you there will be no pop quizzes or essay questions or any blue books or #2 pencils needed when you finish this book. But, you may consider picking up our crib sheets . . . just in case.

A Minor Word About Majors

or

"What Kind Of Job Can You Get With *That*?"

You asked friends, you badgered parents. You bothered professionals and annoyed roommates. You questioned professors and searched your soul for a full two years as an undeclared, the academic equivalent of being in limbo, so that you could accurately decide on a major. A decision changed at least 15 times in the following three weeks. When you ultimately decided that a major in Slavic languages and a minor in forestry was for you, the rest of college became a piece of cake.

Finally, after following a particular course of study, one which you thought would best prepare you to face the challenges of the real world (see previous definition), you began to realize just how far out in left field you've been for the last four years. Nevertheless, armed with your degree and your undying optimism (often mistaken for an ego problem), you find out just how many synonyms there are for the word "unqualified." Herewith, a sampling of popular majors and how they relate to real life.

Philosophy:

What is a job? Will one bring me happiness? What is true happiness? Why are some jobs odd jobs? Are others even? What must I do to receive welfare? Are food stamps for mailing or eating? Where does head cheese come from? What is simonizing, and how does it affect my car? Are Simon and Martin Izing related? Why can't I get a job? Getting the point? Note: Many great philosophers have been known to do stand-up comedy on the side to make ends meet.

Psychology:

With a psychology degree you will clearly understand your anxiety before the interview, the interviewer's decision not to hire you, and your parents' motivation when they nominate you as this year's poster child for birth control. Furthermore, if you are an attractive female fresh out of college and desperate for a job, we suggest showing any potential male employer a little Freudian slip. Who knows, you may look like his mother.

Poli Sci:

As a political science major, your degree qualifies you to own and operate a small country. You would be responsible for keeping the masses impoverished, squandering foreign aid and leading a parade to the unveiling of a bronze statue erected to celebrate your unexpected and miraculous election, as the true leader of your people.

Sociology:
Having just completed four years of intensive study in the values and norms of society, it should come as no surprise that a sociology degree has no value and the norm is not to hire sociology majors. You're dynamite at malls, parties and airports, but tend to take up space in the office.

Geography:
Not since Atlantis sank have there been such opportunities for geography majors. And as long as the continents continue to shift, the demand will persist. The two big fields opening up today are in selling maps to the stars' homes in Beverly Hills, and planning family vacation trips across the country for AAA.

Theology:
Contrary to popular belief, the major issue still baffling the great religious minds of today is not whether the world was created in seven days, did Noah's Ark have a cruise director or was the big bang a "by invitation only affair" and who catered. It is, rather, does one need a theology degree to qualify one's bedroom as a house of worship for

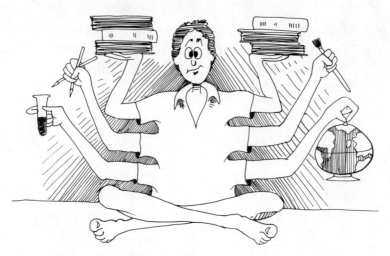

tax purposes. Furthermore, it has been suggested that neither Moses, Jesus, Mohammed nor Charles Manson had valid religious credentials.

So what does a would-be Theologian do without close ties and/or relative status to any recognized Creator? Well, if they're smart, they'll begin to be nonchalantly announcing at an impromptu press conference that God drops by regularly for Sunday Brunch. Then they form a back-up group with a name like "The New Young American Virgin Minstrals—Tra La." From there, plans should be finalized for a Christmas special in the Holy Land, or a studio backlot in Hollywood, California. Whichever provides a more festive atmosphere.

Oh, and remember, scruples, morals and ethics will not be permitted while any miraculous healings, fund raising or raising of the dead is in progress.

Communications:

As a communications major, not only can you clearly express your goals to a potential employer, but also you will grasp the inference behind such phrases as:

- That position has been filled.
- We'll keep your resume on file.
- We're looking for someone with more experience.
- Call us in six months.
- Next time get references other than your parents.

Physics:

With regard to physics majors, the basic principle behind the old joke about the 800-pound gorilla sleeping wherever it wants to applies. The physicist who understands the principles of how to make an atomic bomb, and stands even the most remote chance of locating some plutonium, bunks with the gorilla.

Theater Arts:

When William Shakespeare wrote "All the world's a stage," he must have been in a coffee shop. For the serious theater arts major, the only proven path to stardom is to jump right in. Let those producers and directors know you're available by making a name for yourself right away. Remember, everyone must start at the bottom. There's nothing wrong with being a dishwasher. Soon, bit parts as a busboy may come your way. And if you're lucky, one magic night the Maitre d' will break a leg and you'll be called to stand in. Chase that dream. Don't ever give up. And remember, always serve from the left.

Art/Art History:
You could have been a critic, but you took English pass/fail. You know where all the major works of art are located, but are too busy trying to pay back your student loans to make it to Europe to see them. However, you are a whiz on getting the brown wedgee in Trivial Pursuit™ and we understand there is big money available if you can draw "Skunky" exactly as they do on the back of matchbook covers.

Business:
The exciting world of business is always looking for fresh young minds, that is if you can type at least 60 words per minute and make coffee. If not, go back and get your MBA. The exception is for accounting majors. You will probably be making a small fortune and have little need for this book. Unless you use it to test your new paper shredding machine and write it off as a business expense.

English:
What be wrong with this sentence? What be wrong is you're reading it and not out working at a real job. As an English major, teaching and

writing are about your only two options. Writing may be the only reputable profession which pays less than teaching. The advantage to being a writer is that few professions provide as dramatic and sympathetic an image as the starving writer. It also never fails to impress a date. A starving teacher on the other hand is not a pretty sight. And, passing out in front of a group of fourth graders may give the school board reason to offer you more than just summers off.

So This Is Real Life

or
"I Didn't Spend $50,000 For You To Be A..."

Summer! Ah, the halcyon days of June . . .the sight of string bikinis and Speedos jogging along the beach . . . the smell of freshly mowed grass . . . the sounds of "play ball," the crack of the bat and the roar of the crowds . . . the essence of summer.

All year long you sit in classrooms and daydream about the carefree days and relaxing nights that are summer vacation. The clambakes on the beach, the barbecues in the backyard, the weenie roasts at Camp Okeefenokee. Those family vacations driving across the country in the old station wagon, squashed between Grandpa, who has been carsick since Kansas, and Grandma, who's been playing requests on her false teeth since Nixon resigned.

Does the word "memories" mean anything to you? It should, because that's what these are. Memories, as the song says, "light the corners of your mind," because there they will stay. No longer will you be able to enjoy any of this! At least not with a guilt-free conscience or at your parents' expense.

Your last major decision before leaving college may be . . . what to do with your summer? Just getting out of the house without Mom or Dad throwing the want ads in your Froot Loops begins to feel like Indiana Jones escaping from the Temple of Doom. And this is only one pitfall you will encounter. Basically, you've got three options to choose from:

1) Land a summer job.

2) Go away on a trip.

3) Find a real job.

The decision is yours. We are here only to guide you.

Choice number one, taking a summer job similar to the ones you've had in previous summers, is probably your parents' least favorite. This is because they don't fully appreciate the irony of a $50,000 college degree in the hands of a head fry cook at the local burger stand, a camp counselor or a parking lot attendant.

While you look upon this time as your last hurrah, your parents will most likely view it as a waste of time, and an indication of your immaturity. Go figure!

However, if you are determined to spend your last summer in this fashion, here are some things you should keep in mind:

1) Be sure you leave the house before your parents wake up. Then, stay out until you know they are asleep. (Also, make your bed. No need to add insult to injury.)

2) Never ask them for money. Make sure your job will cover your expenses. Asking for money from parents is like asking them for a thirty-minute lecture about how the money tree died when you went to college.

2b) Stay away from volunteer work.

3) Do not take a job in which you run even the most remote risk of encountering any of your relatives. This will definitely be used against you at the family Fourth of July picnic, where you can hear your Aunt Ethel say, "Since when do you need a college degree to sell toaster ovens?"

4) Never bring home friends who are currently employed at a real job. (Would Custer have given more arrows to the Indians?)

5) Always adhere to the "Rule of Last." Never finish the last piece of pie. Never eat the last scoop of ice cream. Never drink the last beer. Never return the car with an empty tank and never, but never, leave an empty roll of toilet paper in the bathroom. Remember the old adage, "He who finishes the last, won't last."

Option number two, traveling, is perhaps the only one which may afford a demilitarized zone between both warring factions. While the graduates spend their days carousing and frolicking their way through the colorful landscapes of Europe, the parents remain at home. There, they are safe and secure in the knowledge that their child is continuing to pursue culture and education, and, further relieved that said graduate will be away for at least another few months.

This should also be an excellent indication to the insightful college graduate as to just how desperate your parents are to keep you out of the house. The discerning graduate will use this information, and possibly parlay it into an apartment, the keys to the summer house or time on the yacht.

If you have decided to travel, it is important to note that careful planning should be used when considering a destination. With regard to parent complacency, some locations are more effective than others. For example, Hawaii symbolizes fun in the sun, beach blanket romance and all the beer you can guzzle. On the other hand, a more sedate, bleak and intellectual image comes to mind when you are packing for five fun-filled weeks behind the iron-curtain, watching Czechoslovakian farmers herd their yaks.

Here are a few destinations that fulfill the demanding requirements of both students and parents:

•**Greece:** The cradle of civilization. This is a trip that would make any parent proud. Ouzo, the official breakfast drink of Greece, has been known to make many a graduate forget 3000 years of civilization, the word "civilized" and why they are waking up in their underwear in the Acropolis to the sound of a Japanese tour group.

•**England:** Home of pomp, circumstance and a proud history of royal debauchery. Be sure to visit the historical homes of Winston Churchill, the Queen Mother, Sherlock Holmes and Jack the Ripper. Send a postcard home from the House of Lords and The London School of Economics. They are available in most of London's more fashionable pubs.

•**Switzerland/Holland package:** Switzerland, the country that gave us Swiss clocks, Swiss chocolate, Swiss bank accounts, the Swiss army knife, Swiss cheese and yodeling. For the business major this international center of finance is truly a unique place to rub elbows with those wealthy enough to maintain the local banks' minimum monthly balance and afford the service charge. Switzerland offers something for everyone. Fantastic skiing, majestic sightseeing, thrilling mountain climbing, fat men in lederhosen, and its close proximity to Amsterdam.

While Switzerland is famous for its neutral positions, Amsterdam is infamous for more creative positions. Holland, too, has something for everyone: Flowers, hash, windmills, hash, clogs, hash and of course, hash.

•**France:** Paris, The City of Lights and love. It has given us such adorable characters as: deGaulle, Quasimodo, Napoleon, the Marquis de Sade, Louis XIV, Sartre and Richelieu (better known as the seven dwarfs), and, lest we forget, Marie Antoinette starring as Snow White. So please be careful when accepting rides from strangers. France is not only famous for these fun loving historical personalities, but also for its tourist attractions, such as the

Louvre, the Eiffel Tower, Notre Dame, and Versailles. Not to mention that favorite vacation spot: the Bastille.

After your shopping spree on the Champ-Elysees, be sure to send your parents a three-inch plastic replica of the Eiffel Tower with each of your Visa receipts.

•**The Orient:** Spurred on by Bruce Lee movies, tiny radios, saki, very tiny radios, sushi bars, incredibly tiny radios and Godzilla, Japan has become not only a popular tourist attraction, but also the first retail outlet ever to gain U.N. status. Japan is a country steeped in tradition. Be careful when you steal soap from your hotel, because "Death before Dishonor" is still the prevailing notion. To calm your parents' anxiety, before you board your plane, be sure to find out where your pilot was between the years 1941–1945.

For those who wish to face real life (see definition) option number three, finding a job, may be just the thing. Unfortunately, we have always considered employment much like a fine food. A delicacy if you will. It's an acquired taste, much like escargot. And not for just anybody. So, while not qualified firsthand to comment on the joys of being employed, we are fortunate to be able to live vicariously through our friends. We get to empathize and experience the joys and sorrows, the ups

27

and downs, the emotional rollercoaster of the nine-to-five work world. Since they are fellow grads and have contributed so generously to our research, we'd like to present some of their thoughts on being employed.

"Call my secretary, she'll set up a lunch."
—B.Z. Guyy

"If you want to talk to me, call my shrink."
—Noah Home

"Too stressed out to answer."
—Homer Atwork

"Didn't return our phone calls."
—Rich Mann

"On the lam. Jumped bail for white collar crime."
—Ida Nowit

"Presently a hostage in a hostile corporate takeover."
—G.E. Filterfish

We encourage you to take your time and weigh seriously each of the options presented here. After you have considered the advantages and disadvantages of each, choose option two —the vacation. If the economics aren't there to support two, choose option one—the summer job. If, and only if, you are forced to pick three—the real job — close your eyes, take a deep breath, click your heels together three times and say "There's no place like grad school."

The 20-Minute Welcome Home

or
"We're Doing This For Your Own Good . . ."

Regardless of what decision you made in Chapter 2, the harsh reality is, that you are now sitting in the family station wagon on your way home. However, you are not alone. You are accompanied by all of your earthly belongings, including an impressive collection of beer bottles from around the world, and a record breaking three years of unwashed laundry sitting upright beside you entertaining your little sister with cheap card tricks.

Be forewarned, over the past four years while you were away at school, something in your house has changed. No longer is it the place where you would wake in the morning to the smell of sizzling bacon and the sound of flapjacks whizzing through the air. Dad no longer plays football on the front lawn on Saturday afternoons. Something evil has moved in while you were gone. Mom has reached

31

menopause. Dad has lost not only his hair but also $20,000 in bad investments. The paint-by-number picture of Coco the Clown that you once used as a dartboard has been replaced by a "check out time is noon" card, and a request for extra towels can be grounds for additional charges. Your resident status has been downgraded to temporary guest. Anything you say or do can and will be used against you at the dining room table.

For those of you planning to move on quickly, surviving this ordeal is common. For the rest of you who did not bother planning ahead . . . does the Amityville Horror ring a bell? If you do not get out soon, your guest status can be reassessed and before you know it, you'll be redefined as domestic help. This process begins with what psychologists have termed *The 20-Minute Welcome*. A typical scenario sounds like this:

GRADUATE: Ah, it's good to be home.
MOM: Well, it's nice to have you home, dear.
GRADUATE: I'm starved. What's for dinner?
DAD: Mom made your favorite. Linguini with clam sauce.
GRADUATE: Great, maybe tomorrow night we could have lamb chops.
DAD: Now son, your Mother is not your maid. You're gonna have to pitch in around here. Tomorrow I want you to drop me off at work at eight and then take the car in.
GRADUATE: But Dad, I just got home and it's

my first day to sleep in.

DAD: Sleep in?! Tomorrow is Monday. You should be pounding the pavement. Don't you have any job interviews lined up?

GRADUATE: I just finished two grueling weeks of finals. Give me a break.

DAD: There are no "breaks" in the real world. You kids today want everything handed to you. When I was your age . . .

Yes, the twenty minute welcome. However, in fairness to parents, don't misinterpret their actions. They do still care about you. After all, you are a $50,000 investment. It is just that after putting up with you for eighteen years and then enjoying four years of freedom, that cute little body that was once bathed in the kitchen sink no longer fits in as easily as it once did. The little kid who used to sleep 18 hours a day is now expected to wake at the crack of dawn. What was once innocent running around naked in the front yard, is now a misdemeanor. So if it seems the house got smaller while you were away, your perception is somewhat correct. Your house did not get smaller. Your world grew bigger.

WELCOME HOME GRADUATE!

Help Wanted

or
"I Hear Aunt Sally's Brother's Cousin's Husband Is Looking For Someone. Why Don't You Call?"

The time has come to find a job. The one thing college did not prepare you for. To everyone but a philosophy major, now comes the moment in which you discover that you are not the center of the universe. In fact, no employer even knows you exist. (At this point, you may be doubting it yourself.) There are many alternatives, but you did not go to college to be an alternative. And so, the quest begins.

There are several different avenues you may travel in your journey down the highway of success. However, before this starts sounding like a travel guide instead of a survival guide, here are some potential job sources to help you map out your eventual road to employment.

Family and Relatives:

Since these are the people who benefit most from your getting a job and moving out of the house, we suggest taking advantage of them first. While the family bond may make getting the job easier, it also carries its own inherited disadvantages. The biggest disadvantage is the amount of praying you must do. You pray that the fifty dockworkers you oversee will never discover what nepotism means. You pray that your new position as bank vice-president does not involve more math than is needed to tip at lunch. And you pray that your vast experience with your Visa and Mastercard have prepared you to become the head buyer for Daddy's chain of department stores. While working for your family may not be the ideal situation, it can provide a cushion as you adjust from your 11 to 2 class schedule, to the more rigorous 9 to 5 required in the real world.

Friends:

Friends are people who have your best interest at heart, so feel free to capitalize on these relationships. The first step is to find a friend whose job you would enjoy having. Then, show your friend how to make three times the salary by applying that creative energy in a more entrepreneurial fashion. Once he is lulled into the delusion that he can run his own business, leak word to his boss, and . . . POOF! You're on the commuter rail to your brand new job.

Want Ads:

The easiest and most popular method of locating jobs is the classifieds or want ads in your local paper. What a great place to find 1500 employers looking especially for you. Unfortunately, there are 16,000,000 other applicants looking for them. A nice place to look, but you wouldn't want a job from there.

Obituaries:

It should become part of your daily ritual to check the funeral announcements. While it may seem morbid and uncouth, someone has to fill those newly vacated jobs, and it might as well be you. If you do get a job, send flowers—it might relieve the guilt.

The Business Section:

For all you business majors, the business section of the newspaper is a cornucopia of information. You just have to know where to look. For example, the domino theory proves that a recent promotion leaves an opening in the company. Any companies recently added to the Fortune 500 must be doing well and are probably just egotistical enough for you to parlay a barrage of compliments into a high paying corporate position. Finally, watch the real estate section for companies that are expanding. This additional space is not meant to store toxic waste or elves clothing in the off-season. Get the hint?

Employment Agencies:
Let's be serious. If you can't find a job, what makes you think someone else can find one for you.

The Armed Services:
Do you dream about visiting far off exotic places run by malevolent dictators? Do you enjoy dressing like shrubbery? Can you ignore the sounds of gunplay while dining out? If you can, why not work for Uncle Sam and "be all that you can be." Leave the ranks of the unemployed and join "the few, the proud, and those who are first to run up the beach of a hostile country under heavy mortar fire."

For those of you who favor the more creative approach, may we suggest the following:

1) Dressing up as Gumby or Bugs Bunny to get attention and standing in a busy intersection handing out your resume. A sandwich board has a similar effect.

2) Skywriting is a viable option, unless you live in Manhattan where you can't *see* the sky due to the skyline; Los Angeles, where there isn't a sky due to the smog; Chicago, where the wind will keep you unemployed; Miami, where you will have to write in Spanish. Viable is a relative term.

3) Renting a billboard on a major thoroughfare can be effective. Although it also alerts all of your friends and relatives that you are desperate for work, despite your air of confidence.

4) For a more personal approach, consider wrapping and mailing yourself to a potential employer. Even if you don't get the job, at least you will have gained firsthand knowledge of U.S. Postal Service operations. For the deeply desperate, consider Federal Express—"when you absolutely, positively have to be there overnight."

5) To meet the masses in a hurry, may we suggest dropping a thousand of your resumes from a tall building in a major metropolitan area. Don't forget to attach your cover letter.

At this point, "Initiative 101" seems like a more valuable course than "Political Anarchy and the Early Greek Poet." Unfortunately, Initiative 101 was offered at 8 a.m. and the irony only now becomes apparent.

We do not profess that any of our suggestions will work for you. Take it from us. We know. The point is that you are only limited by your own creativity and aggressiveness, for that is what will get you a job.

Getting In The Door, Window Or Executive Washroom

or

"Mom, Where Did You Put That Graduation Outfit?"

In the highly unlikely event that you learn of a job for which you are qualified and it is also one you wish to obtain, there are certain formal steps required to succeed.

Firstly, prepare a clear, concise and competent brag sheet, a resume. While you *can* have one done professionally, it will not only cost you an arm and a leg, but odds are it will also not capture and project the most impressive "you." This is due to the ethics, which unfortunately, prevent the resume writers from lying. However, being a college graduate, it is a safe assumption that you are quite capable of preparing a fine resume of your own. Even if you did take English 101 pass/fail, twice. By simply following the sample resume we provide here and inserting the appropriate personal information, you should be well on your way to getting that first interview. If not, lie. After all, what do you want to be in life? A resume writer.

43

G.E. Filterfish
5555 Kant Drive
Incompetence, Missouri, 41316 } *Accuracy counts here!*
(012) 555-3665

PROFESSIONAL OBJECTIVE: *Be descriptive!*

To obtain a blannd, humdrum position that will fully
utilize my vast professional and educational background.

SUMMARY OF QUALIFICATIONS:

Superior office skills, including: dialing and answering
phones, sitting/sleeping in chair, opening and closing
of doors and locating office

WORK EXPERIENCE:

*← Don't hold back--
If you've got
it, flaunt it!*

Past   Ma and Pa Filterfish Home
4 years   Cheddar, Wisconsin

SON/HOUSEBOY

Responsibilities included: Responding to a
variety of pronouns such as: "Hey you, there";
annd "Now Noodle Noggin, right now!";
bathing on a regular basis;
and serving as butt for family ridicule and scorn.

Reason for leaving: Lost in shuffle of divorce.

Summer   Career Guidance Corporation
Employ-   Idunno, Idaho
ment
                                *Don't be afraid
                          ← to use fancy titles!*

EXECUTIVE ~~SECRETAR~~ SCAPEGOAT

Duties included: Licking and opening envelopes,
achieved stamping status after only three months;
sharpening pencils; picking up inventory from
doughnut cart; being sent out on errands fxx for
no reason;

Reason for leaving: Unsuccessful takeover due to
lack of interest.

EDUCATION: Attica Prison Extension Courses
             x A.A. in Sensitivity Therapy and
             Riot Coordination
             Correspondence courses taken: Acting and Skydiving

REFERENCES: Encyclopedia Brittanica, Webster8s Dictionary

Some other categories you might want to include, if you don't have the vast experience and backround of our Mr. Filterfish: Interests and hobbies; travel experience (prison sentences may be included); languages spoken (English is a given); personal information such as height, weight, color of eyes, any extra limbs; marital status; health; close relatives in high government positions; any relative with "family" ties; and how much overtime you are willing to put out to get ahead in the job.

Once you have compiled the perfect, attention-grabbing resume it's time to get ready to handle the numerous job interviews it will bring. Anyone who has ever told you to not be nervous before a job interview has obviously never had one. They are absolutely terrifying and designed to be so. Knowing that everyone else is equally frightened and unprepared may not calm your nerves, but should alert you to the many practical uses of tranquilizers.

Corporations are known for their use of stress interviews. If the tranquilizer wears off and you find yourself in the midst of a stress interview, remember these helpful points:

1) Never comment on the decor of the interviewer's office. His ex-wife was a decorator specializing in Early American Amish.

2) Offer to lead the Pledge of Allegiance before the interview begins.

3) If offered a cigarette, check for an ashtray first. Interviewers can be so tricky.

4) If in the interviewer's office there is only one chair and it is taken, suggest holding the interview in the executive lounge.

5) Even if the picture of the boss's son or daughter on the desk looks familiar, never mention it. They may not have had the same fond memories of you.

6) If you are asked back for a second interview, we recommend attending. Statistics show that those who do not show up when called greatly diminish their chances of securing the job.

7) Key phrases to refrain from using: Sexual harrassment; insanity in the family; never convicted; Mondale/Ferraro; the doctors say I'm cured; my Father is with the S.E.C.; E.P.A. stats show; and we are the world.

8) Key phrases to use: Money is secondary, it's quality I'm after; Gee, I've never thought about working for anyone else; Isn't that a coincidence, so is my father; I hope you don't mind, I like staying late; I guess you could say I'm married to my work.

What's important is to just be yourself. If the interview is not going as planned, then become someone you think would get the job. And remember, for those of you with weak stomachs, throw up your breakfast before the interview, to avoid any potentially embarrassing situations.

The Gift of Cable

or
"I'll Do It During The First Commercial . . ."

Many people assume that simply because you are unemployed, life is a breeze. That your days are spent lying poolside, sipping Margaritas, reading and highlighting passages from the most recent Harold Robbins paperback. It is these same individuals who are often shocked to discover that the schedule of an unemployed person is so strict and demanding that it is often compared to that of a busy executive fending off a hostile takeover.

After reviewing numerous submissions of the professionally unemployed, we offer this composite schedule to illustrate our point. Feel free to use this schedule as a basis for your own, or clip it and keep it by your bedside. We recommend making copies to distribute to friends and family in response to the barrage of questions about how you spend your day.

A.M.

8:00 Hear Dad's car pull out of the driveway and realize you are safe for another day

8:05 Toy with the notion of getting out of bed

8:06 Ignore notion and roll over

8:10 Mother's vacuum is not as easily ignored

8:15 Alarm goes off (Hey, who set that?!)

8:16 Alarm clock achieves warp speed, but travel is abruptly halted by wall

8:20 Personal hygiene: Brush teeth with shaving cream, apply makeup with comb, run a razor through your hair, spray hair spray under arms, deodorize hair

8:30 Shower (No hot water!)

8:31 All clean

8:32 Attempt to coordinate wardrobe for day's activities, or wear whatever is on the floor from yesterday

9:00 Review newspaper, in particular, sports, Doonesbury and Dear Abby

9:15 Glance at want ads that Father has strategically taped to Trix box

9:30 Ask Mom what is for breakfast

9:31 Catch the broom Mom throws at you

9:32 Breakfast begins: Classic Coke, cold pizza, Pop Tarts with peanut butter and anything still recognizable as one of the four original food groups is fair game

10:00 Say Good Morning to Pat and Vanna as you continue your education on the "Wheel of Fortune"

10:30 "The Jetsons–Speed Racer–Kimba" hour

10:45 "The Jetsons–Speed Racer–Kimba" hour is interrupted by any one of a number of nosy relatives or friends inquiring as to whether you got a job yet

11:00 Open account at bank for free Toaster Oven

11:20 Pawn Toaster Oven

11:30 Insure your future financial success and

support the quality of education by buying a lottery ticket

P.M.

12:00 Check job board at supermarket as you pick up lunch fixings

12:30 Lunch: A six-pack of Lean Cuisines™ and Fudgesicles. You still want to maintain that trim figure for job interviews. During lunch, watch "All My Children" and wonder why Greg and Jesse continue to fight for fatherhood over Natalie's aborted child, and why on "One Life To Live" Vikki is suing Nikki for slander when they are the same person

1:30 Call any working friends who are still on lunch break

2:00 With newfound energy from lunch, wash and detail car (It's amazing how much dirt builds up overnight.)

3:00 "Donahue": You couldn't miss Phil, after all any discussion on how Black-Jewish-Gay and Lesbian couples handle their pregnant, alcoholic, Spanish speaking, college dropouts who plan on becoming taxidermists, should be watched.

4:00 Consider sending out job resumes—tomorrow (Besides, you have already missed today's mail.)

4:05 Decide on excuses for why you did not do the errands your mom asked you to

4:15 Boredom sets in . . . rearrange the bottles in the medicine chest according to expiration dates

4:30 Fulfill family obligation by trying to help little brother with math homework

4:35 Fulfill other family obligation by spending quality time with little brother and Fred Flintstone

5:00 Dad pulls up (Where has the day gone!?)

5:15 Help Mom set table for dinner to alleviate guilt and win her to your side in fights with Dad

5:30 You have been up since 8:00 a.m., you have watched four hours of television and gone to the market. Now comes Miller time. Yes, you've got the time, you've got plenty of time, but do you really want to drink that last beer? (See the Rule of Last—chapter 2.)

6:00 Dinner time (The daily interrogation begins!)

7:00 Drive Mom to the mall in hopes of parlaying it into some new albums

8:00 It's prime time and all three networks are showing a "Wild Kingdom" retrospective. So, get down on your hands and knees and thank the Lord for cable. Tonight it's ROCKY VII in which Rocky battles the Rockettes for copyright infringement.

10:00 Your inquiring mind wants to know if Adam and Eve were space aliens, so you read the Enquirer

11:00 Uh-oh, a rough decision: Flip between reruns of "Taxi," "M*A*S*H" and "Saturday Night Live"

11:30 Take advantage of the fact that long distance is cheaper after 11:00 and call your old college buddies.

A.M.

12:15 Pre-Dave snack: Rocky Road ice cream, nachos and cherry Slurpees

12:30 Dave Letterman—more fun than unemployed college graduates should be allowed to have

1:30 I want my MTV

2:00 You begin seeing close friends in Tom Petty's video (It's time to go to sleep.)

For those of you who do not feel up to such a demanding schedule, we encourage you to start slowly. In time, we are confident that your stamina will increase and enable you to develop a schedule suited to your needs. Then, you too can become one of this great nation's successfully and professionally unemployed.

Odd Jobs And The College Ego

or
"There's Only One Place You Can Go . . . Up!"

On graduating from college, you not only receive a calligraphied piece of parchment, but also something known as "the college ego." The college ego is the condition that prevents the graduate from accepting the first paying job that comes along . . . and the second and the third. This is because the college ego puts each potential job into what is known as the embarrassment equation. This means that each facet of a job is assigned a point value, ranging from 1 to 10, with 10 being most embarrassing. If the ego rejects the job because the point value is too high, it might be easier to just go back and get a different degree.

To save our dear readers the time and effort of evaluating each opportunity as it comes along, both in terms of immediate and long-range personal humiliation, here is a list of job requirements and their relative value in embarrassment equation terms:

- Work uniforms that include wearing a large plastic pepperoni pizza hat 7
  Friends see you wearing pizza hat 8

- Pooper Scooper product tester 5
  Field Pooper Scooper product tester 7
  Promoted to industrial size pooper scooper product tester 9

- Surprise monthly drug tests . . 3
  Caught cheating on drug tests 6
  Not caught cheating and still flunking 8

- Responsible for company copier 2
  You break copier 5
  Caught copying body parts . . 7

For those graduates who intend to use the embarrassment equation, please remember, the better it works, the longer you won't.

The parent who understands that Rome was not

built in a day will also understand that the college ego has taken four years to develop. Four years of constant reassurance and positive reinforcement by both professors and guidance counselors, to cultivate an ego conceited enough to withstand the assault of menial job offers which the lesser ego would welcome and consider appropriate employment.

The parents may have sent you away a mild mannered freshman, but you have returned as . . . SUPEREGO! (Apologies to Freud.) Faster than failing a statistics exam, able to leap library stacks in a single bound and more powerful than the stench after a fraternity party. Here to fight for better pay, shorter hours, stock options and pension plans.

As Superego you have invincible armor which makes you invulnerable to all suggestions, hints and pleas to get a job. However, fear not, for there is an even more powerful force able to bring Superego to its knees; the single thing that Superego needs to survive . . . money!

As Superego's allowance dries up, the plastic reaches its limit, and the car is taken away, Superego is forced to leave your body and search for another innocent, affluent college freshman. The ravaged graduate is slowly returned to an initial humble, unemployed state. Parental patience is rewarded.

Once the graduate is returned to normal, the job pursuit can once again be resumed. Jobs such as dead fish plucker will not only become a curiosity, but also a potential avenue to financial security. There is a wealth of opportunity out there, and the insightful graduate will be able to see through the innocuous job title and appreciate the true potential inherent in each job.

For example:

Mortician's Assistant:

Not only will you strengthen your personal communication skills dealing with these uncooperative people, but you will also gather enough material to write your first book, perhaps a "how to" entitled "Fun With Formaldehyde."

Toxic Waste Maintenance Engineer:

Put your science background to use in the ever expanding and mutating field of nuclear waste clean up. You will gain hands-on experience which will make a glowing impression on any future employer. Job benefits include medical and dental insurance, sprouting new limbs and growing to an enormous size while attacking downtown metropolitan areas.

Underwear Model:

This brief but potentially revealing exposure to the world of high fashion could lead to a lucrative career as a succulent addition to the Fruit of the Loom® bunch. As their grape begins to look more like a raisin, who knows how long it will be before they begin harvesting a new crop of stars.

Parking Violations Officer:
This cushy government job is available to anyone with a background in writing, math and space and time, along with a keen sense of justice. Learn how to wield power effectively while ruining other people's days. The hours are great, 10-12 Monday, 1-4 Tuesday, before noon Friday and weekends off for street cleaning.

Inner-City School Teacher:
If you are the kind of person who believes that the future of tomorrow lies in the dreams of today's children, you might just be gullible enough for this job. For those with any instructional experience and a strong background in hand-to-hand combat, a teaching position may be your key to happiness. With some minor explosives you can

really make an impact on today's youth. Remember, a mine is a terrible thing to waste.

Mime:
In order to become a professional mime, you should have a passion for the arts, a passion for culture and a passion for avoiding foods and beverages being tossed at you by angry mobs. Yes, you will be disliked by appreciative crowds everywhere. Traditional mime dress is stylish, simple and functional. Especially if you are color blind or on your way to a funeral. For those who believe silence is golden, this may be your golden opportunity, and it's a favorite of communication majors.

These are just a few of the many exciting and rewarding career opportunities available to today's college graduate determined to make the most of each job experience. Take a chance. A job is just a job. It's up to you to make it a career. With a little creativity and some hard work, you might just make it. And if you don't, you can always hit the same odds playing the lottery.

Food For Thought

8

or
"If You Think This Is A Restaurant . . . Tip."

Possibly the second most important thing in life is food. Now that you have arrived home, the convenience of a meal plan is a thing of the past. With the potentially cruel situation of having both parents working, managing without a full time chef and with only one entree offered at each meal can be unusually strenuous to the recent college graduate. Thus, it is the goal of this chapter to help you survive those junk food bouts between meals, and the rare dreaded occasion when the parents have the nerve to stay at work late so dinner isn't on the table by 7:00 p.m.

Life isn't always fair, and although it would teach your parents quite a lesson, starving to death at this point could defeat your purpose. Please remember, cooking is a privilege. Do not abuse it. We offer this Seven Day Survival Menu to get you through even the most difficult times.

Use the enclosed recipes sparingly. The Surgeon General has determined that continuous intake of these meals can lead to malnutrition, scurvy, rickets or other diseases pirates get.

SUNDAY: CEREAL

Your clock says 8:00. You're not certain if that's a.m. or p.m., because you spent the first half of the night up with your two good friends, Jim Beam and Johnnie Walker, and the second half of the night praying to the porcelain god. But, you remember how important it is to start your day off right, and it's going to take a lot of sugar to jump start you out of bed this time. There's only one person to turn to. Your childhood pal, Tony The Tiger, he knows just what you need. As long as he doesn't shout, "THEY'RE GRRREAT," you'll make it through another morning.

MONDAY: FROZEN FOODS

In these times of fast food and convenience shopping, perhaps the most useful development in food preparation for the graduate is boxed frozen meals. Today, everything from french bread pizzas to gourmet beef burgundy can be yours in under an hour for about $2.49. So, for the next big date, be a sport and offer to cook dinner. Pop in a couple of Lean Cuisines and be sure you have plenty of time to chill that box of wine. Remember, red goes with Le Menu™, white with Lean Cuisine™ and diet cola with Weight Watchers.™

TUESDAY: POTATOES

You rearranged his face as a child, and later tried to grow one in your kitchen for science class. It's America's favorite side dish and Russia's best loved drink. Of course, we are talking about every child's number one projectile vegetable, the potato. Once dressed for dinner, in their tiny tinfoil jackets, and baked for an hour or so, you have a solid base for an infinite number of meals. In addition, you can boil them, you can mash them, whip them, dice them or salad them, scoop them and scallop them, skin, au gratin, french fry, cottage fry and home fry, julienne, o'brien, casserole, roast, broil, puff, tater tot, hash brown, and best of all, chip them. Even stuffing them isn't a half-baked idea.

WEDNESDAY: THE SANDWICH

Anything put between two pieces of bread is considered to be a sandwich. The sheer number of possibilities in creating and personalizing a sandwich is perhaps its single most inviting feature. The range is awesome. From the ever popular pb&j (that's peanut butter and jelly to the un-hip), to the Monte Cristo (ham, turkey and cheese between two pieces of egg bread, deep fried in batter, sprinkled with powdered sugar and served with raspberry jam by a toothless Hungarian eunuch). The true sandwich connoisseur knows that the height of a sandwich is limited only by the size of one's mouth, and whatever hasn't yet turned green and fuzzy in the fridge.

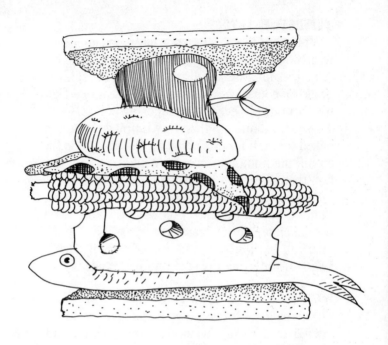

INGREDIENTS

THE CLASSIC
Peanut butter
Jelly
Soft white bread

COLLEGE MEAL
2 slices of Pizza
Flip one on top of another

CALIFORNIA SNACK
Avocado
Tomato
Sprouts
Pita bread

OLD STANDBY
Tuna
Regular potato chips
Crustless egg bread

N.Y. NOSH
Fatty Pastrami
Mustard
Jewish Rye

AUTHOR'S FAVORITE
Sardines
Cream cheese
Onion
Tabasco Sauce
Garlic roll

THURSDAY: MEXICAN FOOD

For those of you with south of the border tastes, who order nachos in French restaurants and always cheered for the Frito Bandito, Mexican cuisine is nino toca. Then again, anything with a little effort and a lot of salsa is nino toca. The true secret to great Mexican food lies not in the ingredients, but in the packaging. Meat or chicken, tomatoes, cheese, lettuce, beans and a shell of some sort, make up 95% of any Mexican meal. The remaining 5% consists of Dos Equis and Coronas. In fact, our mathematics lab has substantial evidence that these 7 items can combine to create over 15 million different tasty delights. Enjoy your meal, but avoid the water. Montezuma was not a kind man, and is still seeking revenge.

FRIDAY: POT LUCK "STOMACH PUMP" DELIGHT

Ever planned an intimate candlelit meal for two and had your little brother show up with 25 sweaty friends for a post-soccer game feast? Knowing that in no time flat, the hungry hoards will be sizing you up for tenderness, you have only one alternative. The Pot Luck "Stomach Pump" Delight. Armed with the largest cauldron you own, nothing in the house is off limits—including the team mascot, Spunky the Wonder Pup.

Remember that fuzzy green stuff in the fridge you didn't want to put in your sandwich two days ago? Toss it in. That brick of edam cheese that has attached itself to the refrigerator door? Pry it off, it makes for an interesting taste. Let the unexpected diners chow down. And for you cooks, may we suggest wearing protective clothing and eyewear.

SATURDAY: CHINESE FOOD

For those of you who know that moo goo gai pan was not a 15th century Chinese emperor, and can tell the difference between Peking and Daffy Duck, the mysteries of Chinese food will delight you. Confuscious say: Chinese food is best when eaten from carton while seated on floor.

If you find the rumor that you are hungry shortly after you eat is true, get double orders of rice, noodles and almond cookies . . . they're free. So for those of you who've never tried it, go ahead and take a wok on the wild side.

SPECIAL NOTE: THE MICROWAVE

The microwave is perhaps the most vital appliance in the kitchen. While appliance jokes abound, the microwave is the sacred cow of the college graduate. For example: It's Monday morning at 7:45 and you have a job interview at 8:00. You haven't eaten since Friday and if you don't soon, passing out on the interviewer's desk will become a distinct possibility. The only thing in the house are some frozen pancakes, but you'll never make it on time. And then you remember . . . God's gift to those who oversleep regularly. The microwave! You could have a five course turkey dinner in under two minutes, including travel time to the store and carving.

Creative grads have adapted the versatile microwave to suit their own needs. In fact, it's not unusual to see groups of them reclining in front of an open microwave in an attempt to rekindle that glowing summer tan. Or to see a romantic couple cuddled together watching their clothes dry with a radioactive tingle and pine fresh scent.

Yes, microwaves should take their place of honor on that illustrious list of student conveniences, along with; a directory of pizza places that deliver, Pink Floyd's "The Wall," and a thorough working guide to current social diseases and their cures.

COMBUSTIBLE COMESTIBLES

Now that we have encouraged you to run amok in the kitchen, we feel it is our moral duty to warn you about certain food items to stay away from. (Unless, of course, you are preparing the Pot Luck Stomach Pump Delight.) These include: Anything growing unnaturally (mint chip ice cream which was formerly vanilla), anything that shies away from your touch, anything you cannot classify in one of the basic food groups, things still alive, except sushi and yogurt, anything that offers to grant you three wishes if you do not eat it, potatoes with more eyes than the Vienna Boys' Choir, anything with the word "surprise," "delight," or "new and improved," (You have to wonder what was wrong with it the first time, and how do you know they got it right this time?) and anything needing to be microwaved for more than two hours probably wasn't meant to be eaten in the first place.

While this culinary crash course will not make you the Galloping Gourmet, it should allow you to fumble through any meal, even if it means breaking new ground and going where no chef has gone before. The Burger Stable. Home of the 1/4 pound jockey burger. It may be little, but it's sure to give you the trots. Let's face it, even Julia Child and Betty Crocker had to start somewhere. And you can rest easy, sure in the knowledge that even Sara Lee put too much brandy on her first Cherries Jubilee, singeing her eyebrows and setting off smoke alarms for miles around.

Home Sweet Home

or
"It's What They Call A 'Fixer Upper'"

Eventually, sooner or later, at some point, there will come a time, sometime, when you will actually consider, think about, wonder and ponder, the possibility of moving into your own place. Maybe. And, it is with this type of determination, fervor and zeal for independence that you must attack the task of moving out. While moving out may be something you've looked forward to ever since the 20 minute welcome, finding a suitable dwelling in many of our major cities can be a veritable nightmare on Elm Street. Not only do you need a small fortune and some serious family money to cover the first, last, middle, key, cleaning, and security deposits, but you need a linguistics degree to read the local apartment listings.

Compiled herewith is a list of abbreviations most likely to frustrate and undermine you in the pursuit of your independence, maturity and your very own HOME SWEET HOME.

A/C	air conditioning
ba	bath
bel	broken elevator
bi/lvl	bi-level
bu/in	built-ins
CAC	central air conditioning
ckrinf	cockroach infested
cfwy	condemned for freeway
CJ adj	County Jail adjacent
cont	contemporary
das	directly above subway
d/w	dishwasher
el	elevator
fbp	frequented by police
fpl	fireplace
f/t	firetrap
furn	furnished
g/d	garbage disposal
hrdfl	hardwood floor
lvstk	zoned for livestock
naw	no automatic weapons
nhw	no hot water
nls	no loud sex
npdr	not in pizza delivery range
nw	nymphomaniacs welcome (see manager)

ph	penthouse
pkg	parking
pt gar	private garage
sec	security
th	townhouse
unf	unfurnished
vln	very loud neighbor
vu	view
w/d	washer and dryer
wta	walk to airport
w/w	wall to wall carpeting

Now that you've had a chance to familiarize yourself with the glossary, try your hand at deciphering the classified ad below. Captain Midnight decoder rings and Rosetta Stones are considered cheating.

CALL-CALL-CALL-CALL-CALL-CALL-CALL-CALL-CALL APT 4 RENT:

$3+2+1+\frac{1}{2}=6\frac{1}{2}$; b/u; w/w; w/d; d/w; r-e-s-p-e-c-t; htd pl; rec room; pkg gar; g/d; unf; cont; M-O-U-S-E. $825/mo. Call Bob.

Now that you've learned how to locate an apartment you've got one small problem . . . it's commonly called rent.

At this point, you are faced with two options. The first is to stay at home, and try to convince any date you have that you're really a Swedish exchange student who is only visiting with this family. The second is to find a discerning individual lucky enough to live with you. After all, you are charming, courteous, considerate, witty, fastidious and soon to be canonized. Quickly discounting the first option because you can't fake the Swedish accent, you decide to find a roommate.

When searching for a potential roommate, there are three important criteria. Each one should be applied while screening candidates.

1) The ability to pay the rent—We suggest checking the family tree. Important clues may be found in the following surnames: Kennedy, Rockefeller, Iacocca and Vanderbilt. Lacking a suitable last name, try walking the prospective roommate out to his or her car. If you end up at the bus stop, keep looking. If you arrive at a red Ferrari, check for rental plates.

2) Compatibility—By "compatibility," we do not mean that you would kill or die to see the person in his or her underwear. We refer to sharing common morals, ethics, and values. Of course if none of these are present, seeing a person in skivvies may be a worthwhile option.

3) Are they housebroken? Not the roommate so much as the pets. By pets, we don't mean hamsters, gerbils and other non-life threatening critters. We're talking about dobermans, boa constrictors named "Sweetums," or barnyard animals like sheep. Unless of course, having your apartment zoned for livestock is on your list of things to do.

Now that you know what to look for in a room-

mate, you have to get the word out that you're looking.

In this modern age, there are two words which are best suited to bringing together people who are looking for each other but may not even know it. No, they're not "Dating Game," or even "assault and battery." Try "personal ad." May we suggest the following:

WANTED

Roommate to share apartment. Ideal candidate will not leave hair on soap. Will not wait for nasty warnings from the Board of Health before cleaning room. Will not allow leftovers in fridge the chance to evolve into higher lifeforms. Will not engage in sex loud enough to draw a crowd. Will not attempt to decorate living room in black velvet Elvis posters. The King is dead, and no one looks good in black velvet.

You may have noticed that we left out any mention of moving in with friends. There's a good reason for that. It's just as easy to turn a good friend into a stranger as it is to turn a stranger into a good friend.

Time, Money And Other Things You're Short Of

or

"'Tis Better To Give Than To Receive, But In Your Case . . ."

The first year out of school for a college graduate is always the most difficult. To survive, a certain amount of planning and budgeting is essential.

When you graduate, it is safe to assume that you will receive some cash, as well as other gift items easily convertible to cash. Take a lesson from Mr. Squirrel, nature's little budgeteer, and store some of your nuts away for the winter. In other words, depending on when your birthday is, this initial source of income may have to tide you over until the holidays.

By understanding the ups and downs of your cash flow, you can more effectively avoid those high and dry times when you're tempted to pawn Mom's silverware, or your little brother to the highest bidder. Let the calendar below serve as a reminder of just how quickly the year can go, and how your money loves to tag along with it.

FIRST YEAR MILESTONES

June College graduate fiscal year begins. Cash flow should be no problem.

September You could be back at school beginning a masters program. Rethinking your options sets in.

October Halloween means free candy with potential resale value, and a sugar rush to carry you through to Thanksgiving.

November Thanksgiving is turkey day, but whose goose is cooked when questioning relatives stop by? Wrapped, stored in the freezer and eaten sparingly, the leftovers can tide you over until Christmas.

December Now that the family has labeled you an unemployed bum, console yourself with the knowledge that the gift giving season is here to bail you out and perpetuate that carefree existence you've grown accustomed to.

January	New Year's Resolution: I think I can, I think I can, I think I can get a job . . . if not, I can always go back to bed.
February	Washington's Birthday! Lincoln's Birthday! Valentine's Day . . . and not a single gift! Groundhog's Day—stick your head out of bed, if you don't see an employer's shadow, six more weeks of unemployment.
April	Your friends are off to the sun for spring break, and you're this year's April's fool.
May	Your first year. You made it. Congratulations. Throw a party. If you can't afford it, crash someone else's graduation party.

In addition to these, there are a number of other highpoints during the year which should be included in the recent graduates' annual financial plans. The most important of these is date of birth. If you're lucky, it was a long, cold December, and your parents were feeling frisky one night. In other words, ideally your birthday fell nine months later. Lucky for you, this means your birthday falls during the summer months when holiday gift money is running low and vacation ideas abound.

Other year-round income producing ventures should never be overlooked. And they have the distinct advantage of being things you would do anyway, so they can't really be labeled as odd jobs and risk offending your college ego.

These include:

- Saving aluminum cans, and paper—that case worth of sixers you just finished may put a gallon of gas in the car. Recyclables are our friends.

- Running errands for Mom—change does add up, especially when taking in Dad's laundry.

- Visiting the grandparents as a detour on your dates—most would give their right arms to see you married off, or at least cough up $20 for a good time.

- Entering any and all free sweepstakes—the odds usually aren't very good, but then neither were the odds of you graduating, which goes to show that miracles can happen.

- Entering all radio contests—once you've memorized the phone numbers, practice being the 27th caller.

This chapter can help out but remember, your

next year may not be as easy. So learn the golden rule of business—make all the money you can, spend as little as possible, and don't tip unless people are looking.

College Graduates & Other Hazards Of Sex

or
"Stop Me If You've Heard This . . ."

For those of you who have spent years believing that it is sheer coincidence that all parents sound alike, this chapter will help clarify this misconception. You see, there are three perfectly kept secrets in the world. The first, is what makes up the creme filling in a Twinkie. The second is that Michael Jackson and Diana Ross are the same person (notice that Michael's lips never move when Diana talks). And, the last secret is that all parents attend a secret three day seminar when their children are on the verge of graduating from college.

The seminar, entitled, "How to deal with your college graduate, and other hazards of sex," teaches the anxiety-ridden parents fundamental behavior techniques to use with the returning graduates. The course curriculum is as follows:

DAY 1:

Introduction: A quick trip to the drugstore could have prevented all of this

Putting students in their place ... preferably where they pay the rent

DAY 2:

Letting your child go ... then changing the locks

Guilt as a weapon: An owner's manual

The nuclear family : How to live with a graduate without exploding.

DAY 3:

The child who came to dinner (And stayed!)

To charge or not to charge rent, and other rhetorical questions

Farewell address: Celibacy, the road not taken.

The parents leave the seminar with a renewed sense of authority and hostility towards the returning graduate. They are well prepared to deal with the inevitable assault of the college ego. In addition, they have developed a support group comprised of other parents of grads in the neighborhood.

They say the proof of the pie is under the crust. So for those who still doubt the validity of these claims, what follows is especially for you. It is an authentic list of phrases that must be memorized by every parent before completing the course. It was procured when two young graduates went undercover, at great risk to life and limb, and attended the highly secretive Newark, New Jersey Parents of Graduates (POGS) Seminar. They are still undergoing therapy, and should be on solid food soon.

- "Not under this roof you won't."
- "Allow me to introduce you to the washing machine."
- "What did your mother and I do to deserve this?"
- "I hope you end up with kids just like you."
- "Talk to her, she's your daughter."
- "My house, my rules."
- "What did they teach you in that school?"
- "Whoever said that life would be easy?"
- "Our obligation ended when you turned eighteen."

Fortunately, college graduates can usually defend themselves by retorting with a simple, all encompassing phrase guaranteed to end any discussion.

- "Hey, I didn't ask to be born."

CH-CH-CH-CH-CHANGES

or
"Can I Quote You On That?"

Bob Dylan sings the words, "The times they are a-changing." As you grow older, it is inevitable that things change. Things that were once simple have become complicated. Things that were once complicated still are.

For example, the imaginary friends you hung around with when you were three no longer come around. If they do, we recommend not lending them anything of value. Drinking out of a bottle is no longer a necessity. And if it has become a necessity, it may explain the return of those imaginary friends.

Even words of wisdom that you grew up hearing and repeating take on new meaning to the college graduate. We have compiled some of the more popular phrases that are going around. Study and incorporate them into your daily banter. They will help soften that "wet-behind-the-ears" edge.

- The grass is always greener . . . with a different degree.

- He who hesitates is a philosophy major.

- Hear no evil. See no evil. Speak no evil.— The Lawyers Credo

- He who laughs last is the guy who got the job.

- Honor thy father and mother . . . until you get your own apartment.

- All good things come to those with a master's degree.

- The Lord is my shepherd. I shall not want for anything else, if he gets me this job.

- I shall not commit adultery. Unless it is clearly stated in the job description.

- Give us your tired, your poor, your huddled masses yearning to be employed.—Job Agency motto.

- We the people, in order to form a more perfect union, demand summers off.

- Look before you leap on the boss's wife. He may come home early.

- Never bite the hand that feeds you, clothes you, pays the bills. In fact, get it a manicure.

- Quitters never win, winners never quit, and people who sleep late never get the job.

- The early bird catches the worm. Big deal, can the worm get you a job?

While Bartlett may not appreciate this list, he was probably lucky enough never to have heard Bob Dylan sing either.

AFTERWORD

We hope that you have enjoyed our little humorous critique of being a college graduate. But more importantly, we hope you put this book down having more confidence than when you picked it up. Knowing that just about everyone else, short of computer science majors, is in the same boat. And believe it or not, you too will stay afloat.

While rejection, uncertainty and fits of depression may presently seem to be your three constant companions, enjoy these turbulent times. They're the most fun turbulent times you will ever have. Unless of course you're lucky enough to one day get fired.

Oh, and don't ever lose your most valuable survival skill. The one tool that can turn a screaming parent into a friend, an interview into a happy hour or a boss into a buddy. Your sense of humor. Just remember to give it plenty of exercise, a little extra attention, and its own set of towels.